Top Table

A Satirical Comedy

Margaret Wood

A SAMUEL FRENCH ACTING EDITION

SAMUEL FRENCH

FOUNDED 1830

SAMUELFRENCH-LONDON.CO.UK
SAMUELFRENCH.COM

FOR AMATEUR PRODUCTION ENQUIRIES

UNITED KINGDOM AND WORLD EXCLUDING NORTH AMERICA
plays@SamuelFrench-London.co.uk
020 7255 4302/01

Each title is subject to availability from Samuel French,

depending upon country of performance.

AUTHOR'S NOTE

This play can be performed by an all-male, all-female or a mixed cast. Masks can be used effectively to stress nationality and the element of satire.

Those who may find that some episodes in the play seem exaggerated, may recall that in the Indo-Chinese border dispute, war almost broke out over a few sheep and goats and a piece of linoleum which had strayed across the border: and that the Paris-Vietnam peace conference was delayed for weeks over disputes about the shape of the table. An American plane was shot down inside the Russian border at a most crucial diplomatic moment: and in October 1972 the delicate peace talks between the Vietnamese and Kissinger were imperilled by an ill-timed raid on the French Legation in Hanoi.

CHARACTERS

USSR
USA
UK
India } *Delegates*
Africa
China
First Cleaner
Second Cleaner
Officials
Photographers
Other Delegates

The action passes in a Conference Room

Period – today or any day

TOP TABLE

A conference room

At the back is a long window which appears to open on to a balcony. Outside the window is a suggestion of flags of different nationalities, and above it is a large cut-out of a dove of peace. There is an entrance downstage on each side of the room. In front of the window is the conference table, which is in three separate sections with a space between each

Before the CURTAIN *rises, sprightly music, such as the Clog Dance from "La Fille Mal Gardée", or anything with a well-marked rhythm, is heard. It continues during the following mimed action, which is briskly stylized in precise time to the music*

Two Cleaners, in overalls or clothes which suggest they are menials or low-grade workers, enter from the opposite doors. One carries ashtrays, the other blotting pads. These they proceed to bang down rhythmically before each place, in time to the music. Each disappears by the door opposite to the one by which he or she entered, and almost immediately reappears with trayfuls of name-plates, each inscribed with the name of a delegate country. They place the principal name-plates as follows: on the table down R, *starting down stage—India, Africa, USSR; on the table* C, *which has an ornate "Chairman's chair" behind it, USA; on the table down* L, *UK, China, and an extra. Any other delegates who do not speak can sit behind the two side tables, but not behind the centre table. As soon as the name-plates are placed there is a sound of cheering outside and the music changes to an African beat. One of the Cleaners hurries to the window and looks out. As they announce each nation they turn and speak out to the audience, loudly, in the manner of a compère*

First Cleaner They are arriving! Africa is arriving at the peace conference!

Second Cleaner (*joining the First*) Africa! The emergent nation! Welcome to Africa.

They embrace each other ecstatically, African fashion. Cheers are heard off. The music changes to an Indian theme

First Cleaner India!
Second Cleaner India has come!

They put their palms together and bow formally. The music changes to the "Star-Spangled Banner". Cheers are heard off

First Cleaner America!
Second Cleaner The US of A.

They whip off their caps and hold them over their hearts. The music changes to twanging Eastern notes

First Cleaner
Second Cleaner } China! { *(Speaking together*

They put their hands inside their sleeves and bow to each other. "God Save the Queen" is heard

First Cleaner
Second Cleaner } The United Kingdom! { *Speaking together*

They stand to attention and then shake hands very formally. The "Internationale" is heard

First Cleaner
Second Cleaner } United Soviet Republics! { *Speaking together*

They stand with fist clenched and raised. Prolonged cheers are heard off, dying away in a hubbub of voices

First Cleaner They're coming!
Second Cleaner The Great Peace Conference is about to begin.
First Cleaner
Second Cleaner } Let us open the doors! { *Speaking together*

They fling open the two doors

From each door a Photographer enters backwards, crouching, trying to focus on the delegates who are entering. The cheering and chattering cause them to shout their requests for the first few moments

USSR, Africa and India enter from R, *USA, UK and China from* L, *and any extras from the door nearest their table*

First Photographer Thank you, everybody, thank you. Just one more. (*To China*) Your Excellency, would you mind shaking the American delegate by the hand? Thank you.

There is a flash—China and USA are transfixed in a beaming smile

Second Photographer (*to UK*) Sir, would you embrace our Soviet comrade?
UK (*stiffly*) Well, I'll shake hands.

UK offers to shake hands but is engulfed in USSR's bear-like hug. Bulbs flash

USSR Ah, my dear brother, this is History, and this is us making it.
First Photographer (*to Africa*) And you, sir. Could you give us a picture?
Africa Sure, man, sure. I make lovely picture. Very colourful. Very jazzy.
Second Photographer Now a group. May we have a group, gentlemen? If you will arrange yourselves. . . .

They group themselves against the top table, USA and USSR jostling for the centre of the picture. Hands are gripped and teeth bared in terrifying bonhomie

Smile, please. Chee-eese. That's right. Hold it, hold it.

More bulbs flash and there is much back-slapping as the delegates move to their places

The Photographers and all others except the delegates go out

USSR reaches the centre of the table and reads the USA label. USA arrives at the same moment. USSR takes up his label and exchanges it for USA's. USA picks up his own label and puts it back, replacing USSR's in its original position. USSR repeats his replacement very firmly. Tension is growing when UK intervenes

UK May I suggest that to balance the side tables properly, both the Russian and American representatives should sit at the top table. That would leave an equal number of us at the sides.
USA That's quite a notion. I'll go along with that.

Africa A jolly fine idea, man.
China Okay.
India I'm pretty well totally in agreement with that agreement.
USSR Hurrump. (*He sits grumpily in the ornate chair*)

USA brings his chair round from the side. All sit. There is a pause for a moment, then USA begins to rise

USA Gentlemen . . .

But USSR has shot up quickly, and breaks in

USSR Comrades and friends! My heart is full. We have in Russia a proverb, "When the heart is full, the head is often empty." If that is so, comrades, we have many empty heads round this table today.

Polite laughter

We are not ashamed to own it. Full hearts, and heads empty of all hatred and envy, are needed for the purpose for which we are gathered here. It is with full heart, therefore, that I say, "Brothers, let us get on with fulfilling that purpose." I declare this historic conference open.
USA Say, hold it, brother. Why you?
USSR Why me what?
USA Why should *you* declare the conference open? Have we elected a chairman?
USSR What need for a chairman? We meet in perfect harmony, perfect unity.
USA Not as perfect as all that.
China Please! Protocol must be observed. Only chairman is Chairman Mao.
USSR Chairman Mao not present. I am in the chair. See— (*pointing to the ornate chair*)—Chairman's chair.
China Excuse, please. In absence of Chairman Mao I demand that all chairs shall be equal.
Africa I am delighted to support that honourable fellow's protest. To have big chair is most unfair.
India Sedentary arrangements must be totally on the level.
UK Er—ah—it is usual for the chairman to have a place of importance from which to discipline and control the meeting.
USSR Aah! (*He points accusingly at UK*) Filthy capitalist idea. I agree with the protest of the honourable Asian member.

Remove Imperialist-type chair and supply same as my brother here.

The non-speaking delegates from the ends of the tables quickly exchange the chairs. There is an outburst of clapping as USSR seats himself

Now we are more equal than ever. Shake hands, comrade!

USSR shakes the bewildered USA by the hand. USA puzzles over the fact that he seems to have lost a point without knowing why

As I was saying, today we, the greatest nations in the world, have met to resolve on complete renunciation of all nuclear and other weapons. We have left no stone unturned, no avenue unexplored in our search for peace. And what is the result? Suspicion and fear are at an end.

China (*holding up his Mao's thoughts*) Chairman Mao has a very fine thought on this topic. He say, "To gather round a table is better than to take sides."

General murmurs Sure, sure, hear, hear.

China (*beaming as he sits*) Thought four hundred and thirty-two.

Africa Man! There's an error in logic there. I guess we can't gather round a table that's not round.

India It is in absolutely no respect a round table.

Africa How can we have a round table conference if the table is not round?

India In fact, we find the table unacceptable, my dear fellow.

USA (*ironically*) Waal, fine. That's goddam fine. First the chair, then the table. What is this—an antique fair?

Africa (*firmly*) For round table conference we must have round table.

UK "Round table" is just a manner of speaking, I think.

Africa What about British Commonwealth's Knights of the Round Table? Man, I guess you ain't never done your English "O" level.

UK (*stiffly*) King Arthur's round table wasn't a conference. In any case, the members were usually off somewhere else.

USA Gentlemen, we cannot, in the situation as of now, have a round table conference. It's gotta be an open-ended one—like this set-up.

Africa ⎫
China ⎬ Why? ⎰ *Speaking*
India ⎭   ⎱ *together*

USA Because the Press must sit somewhere.

USSR Where is the Press?

USA (*indicating the audience*) Out there. There's the *Noo York Tribune*, there's *The Times*, there's the *Daily Express* . . .

USSR (*delightedly*) There's *Pravda*! Greetings, Vronsky! Can you hear me, brother?

USA We can't close our circle to make a round table. They'd never hear us.

UK They get everything wrong as it is. I propose that we leave the tables as they are.

USA Agreed.

USSR Agreed.

China I propose that we exchange table right for table left—and vice versa.

USA The hell you do. What difference does that . . .

UK (*sotto voce*) Agree, man. Asiatics mustn't lose face.

USA O.K. Agreed.

The tables are whipped up by the people at each end, rapidly swapped, and the delegates sit as before

USSR Democracy is democracy.

China Many thanks. That is better. Now we get somewhere.

USSR Now at last suspicion and fear are at an end?

India They are?

USSR We trust each other?

Africa Sure, sure.

China I tlust you and you tlust me. This our great leader, Chairman Mao, sings as he swims down the Yangtze.

Africa I would like to sing you a song composed of those beautiful words.

All Later, brother, later.

Africa subsides, smiling broadly

USA What greater proof of trust could you have than those two great armies drawn up in the square outside? Our army of the Eastern hemisphere and yours of the West?

USSR (*to UK*) You British have a saying, "Oh, East is East and West is West and never the twain shall meet. . . ."

UK (*uncomfortably*) That is so. Out of date, of course.

USSR Of course. That is your most charming characteristic. Here, today, your saying is disproved. East and West have met. They face each other across the square, not with fear, not with suspicion, but with trust—and—may I dare to say—with love?

USA (*much affected*) You may, brother, you may.

UK Hear, hear.

India Lovely sentiments, very lovely.

They all clap as USSR sits and USA rises

USA This is an historic moment. Never before in hooman history has the Noo World been in a position to cement, with the—er —milk of hooman kindness, the bonds of friendship with the old. And with that Eastern part of the Old with whom we have not, hitherto, felt a close sense of communion. I refer, of course, to the Soviet Union.

China (*rising*) Excuse, please. I am Eastern nation.

USA (*hastily*) Sure, brother. You certainly are. I meant, of course, to include you in.

China Me small. China velly big.

USA Sure, sure, I . . .

China (*holding up his book, very persistently*) Chairman Mao has a saying, "Sailing the sea of Diplomacy depends upon the helmsman." Thought three hundred and sixty.

USA So what? That's to say, okay, okay. We're great buddies, all of us.

China (*relentlessly*) Chinese people velly numberous. In a good cause we can throw them away. Nobody notice.

USA Not in this cause, brother. It's so durn good that nobody need be thrown away.

Laughter and applause, during which USA sits and UK rises

UK It is with great pleasure that I endorse what other speakers have said. In the past, the New World has been brought in to redress the balance of the Old. Now we need no makeweights. We are in perfect balance, perfect harmony. So, gentlemen, in the words of the immortal bard, "Let me not to the marriage of—er—marriage of—er . . . (*He searches in his notes*)

Africa (*rising*) Allow me.
  "Let me not to the marriage of true minds,
    Admit impediment."
UK (*stiffly*) Thank you.
Africa A pleasure, man. I didn't pass my Cambridge School
  Certificate for nothing.

They sit. Polite applause, while India rises

India I too would like to be adding my felicitations to this lovely
  company. We in India and the other emergent nations are very
  happy to join in this jolly good show and go forward hand
  in hand towards the sunset of a new dawn on which the horizon
  will never set. I, myself, am ready to sign this treaty with my
  very genuine gold fountain pen.
Africa I am also ready to sign this admirable treaty, especially
  as I haven't any nuclear weapons anyway.
China (*meaningly*) Yet.
Africa (*beaming*) Yet.
China So! All is ready.

*There is a pause while USA and USSR and others eye one another
suspiciously*

India In the words of the old song, "Why are we waiting?"
Africa Yes, why? I can, incidentally, give you a fine rendering
  of those words "why are we waiting" while we wait.
All Later, later.
USSR (*clearing his throat*) Are we then ready to sign?
USA (*uncomfortably, looking round*) Well, are we?
UK It appears we are—more or less.

The delegates take up their pens, still warily eyeing one another

USSR In that case . . .

The door opens and an Official rushes in

Official Stop!

USSR lays down his pen—so does everyone else

USSR We have not yet begun.

Official A cable for the delegate from the United States of America!

USA (*reading it*) Almighty Gaard! I must get on the hot line to Washington.

USA turns, but finds his way blocked by UK

UK I say, old man, we're in on this, you know.

USA Will you get outa my hair? Lemme get outa here.

USSR (*laying a firm detaining hand on his shoulder*) Comrade, may I remind you that I too have a hot line?

China Excuse please, me too. I have hot line to Peking. Direct to Chairman Mao as he swims down the Yangtze river.

Africa What is all this palaver? We are ready to sign. Why do we not sign?

India Why do we not strike while the iron is hot?

USA Because it's too bloody hot!

USSR (*exploding*) Because always we are thwarted by non-co-operation by the Western bourgeois filthy capitalist powers. They do not truly desire peace. Always they cause a diversion —a deliberate diversion.

USA (*coming round his side of the table into the middle of the room*) *We* do not desire peace? It is my painful dooty to ask the delegates to listen to this cable. Then tell me who does not desire peace.

USSR Read it, then. I defy you!

USA It says, "American plane shot down near Russian border."

UK (*covering his eyes with his hand*) Oh, no! Not again.

From the opposite side an Official enters with a cable for USSR

USSR Lies! (*He takes the cable and opens it*)

USA Direct from Washington. You are at liberty to investigate.

USSR We shall. (*He reads his cable. His eyes start from his head*) A-a-ah! (*With dangerous silkiness*) Be so good as to read your cable again.

USA "American plane shot down near Russian border."

USSR "Near." Listen now to Soviet cable. "American plane shot down *inside* Russian border."

USA *Lies!* (*He comes into the centre*)

USSR Direct from the border. You are at liberty to investigate.
USA Hypocrite! I come here in all good faith.
USSR (*snarling*) You come here with a pistol disguised as an olive branch.
UK (*coming into the centre*) Gentlemen, gentlemen. I beg that you will do nothing in haste. I propose that we set this matter on one side to be dealt with by a committee of investigation, and proceed with the business of the treaty. The door is still open.
USSR (*turning away impatiently*) Your doors always are.
USA And a bloody great draught blows through them.

An Official enters and hands cable to UK and Africa

Africa That's the wind of change, brother. We know all about that. (*He shares his joke with India, then reads his cable*) By Golly! (*He comes into the centre and shakes his fist at UK*) You have sold us down the river again.
UK I have no idea what you are talking about. (*He reads his cable*)
Africa Do you deny the truth of this? "White racialists in southern Zimbango massacre African natives."

An Official enters with cables for China and India

UK Of course I deny it. My cable says, "Southern Zimbango riots quelled. Peace and order restored."
Africa Lies, lies.
India (*coming forward*) I am exceedingly sorry to interrupt this brilliant debate between my dear old pals, but I find it impossible to sign this eminently desirable treaty. China has invaded our northern frontier.
China (*coming forward*) Lies! Double closser! We have not invaded our northern frontier. You have invaded our southern one. Moreover you have carried off thirty sheep, four goats and a piece of linoleum, in addition to killing three shepherds. The shepherds do not matter. We have plenty people. But thirty sheep! Four goats! Linoleum. This is war.

During this criss-cross argument, speakers "take the stage" in turn, continuing their argument in dumb show when the others take over, perhaps with a circling movement that brings the various couples to the fore in turn

USA (*to USSR*) I'm warning you. You are inviting total destruction. I shall immediately contact the President at the White House.

USSR Do so. But do not forget I can wage wars, and win wars, sitting at this table. My hot line is here. (*He takes what appears to be a fountain pen from his pocket and begins to talk into it*) Double cross five calling double cross one, double cross five . . . etc.

UK (*trying to impede USA's progress towards the door*) If the United Kingdom may mediate in these matters we shall be only too happy to do all in our powers to bring about a peaceful settlement.

USA Who in hell d'ye think you are? A world power or somethin'? And drop all this diplomatic crap.

UK But I assure . . .

USA I'm going out of this room right now to talk to Washington, and if the President sees fit to push the button, so much the worse for everyone.

UK Including you! Don't you see? He's going to press it first. (*He points to USSR*)

USSR Come in, double cross one. Are you receiving me? Good. Operation Mushroom Cloud to take effect at—(*he looks at his watch*)—three hundred hours. Contact all concerned. Over and out. (*To USA*) That gives your major cities about five minutes to blast off.

USA (*pushing UK aside*) Let me get outa . . . (*He strides to the door and finds it locked*)

Meanwhile India and China have been in hot argument

India We have not touched your utterly derisory sheep and goats. Animals are sacred to us. We carry them off only as errand of mercy. Your charge is highly laughable. See, I laugh!

China Thirty sheep no laughing matter. Your action is bourgeois and revisionist.

Africa (*snapping his fingers in UK's face*) Imperialists out! British *out*! White races out, *out*, OUT!

China India *out* . . . etc.

India China *out . . .* etc.

Uproar. Each group now reaches its respective doors and finds them locked

USA Open up, there. Open up, I say!
USSR Unlock this door. The conference and the world are both at an end.

The doors suddenly open and the two Cleaners stand there, each with a gun

First Cleaner Silence!
Second Cleaner Belt up!

There is a moment's astonished silence. Then indignation breaks out

USA Say, what *is* this? Outa my way. This is urgent.
First Cleaner (*waving the pistol under USA's nose*) So is this.
Africa Make way, please.   ⎧ *Speaking*
India We have important business   ⎨ *together*
China I must settle his hashish!   ⎩ *in hubbub*
Second Cleaner Sorry. No exit.
UK What do you mean, my good man? These are doors, aren't they?
First Cleaner Yes. And I am a good man. But not yours.
USA But this is fantastic. Held up by a couple of Mrs Mopps.
UK I say, you know, you can't do this. What are you doing with pistols?
USSR (*shocked*) Don't you know this is a peace conference?
First Cleaner (*sardonically*) We had heard.
USA Say, who let these crackpots in? Why doesn't someone arrest them?
India I personally am not armed. You do it.
UK There are only two of them. Call for help. I say, you chaps out there. He-e-lp!
First Cleaner If you would please to look over our shoulders, you will see that there are more than two of us.

Both groups stand on tiptoe, looking off in each direction

UK Good God! Soldiers—all along the corridors!

USSR (*turning and snarling at USA*) And American uniforms among them.

USA (*thrusting his face into USSR's*) Also Soviet uniforms.

India I am unashamedly delighted to see Indian ones also.

Africa And African.

Second Cleaner And British and Chinese and any other variety you care to mention.

USA (*sitting and mopping his head with relief*) Oh waal! That's O.K. Our men are there.

UK Just for a minute I thought we were trapped.

First Cleaner Well, if you can't get out of here——

Second Cleaner —that's what you are. Trapped.

They advance into the room as they speak, driving the occupants back into the centre

USSR Cannot get out? What nonsense is this you talk? You shall have a short holiday in Siberia for this little prank.

USA What do you think you two can do against the vast armies of East and West which are facing each other across the square outside?

First Cleaner Are they facing each other?

USA You know they are.

First Cleaner Take a look out of the window. Go on, take a look.

USA and USSR go to the window. One Cleaner covers them while the other keeps an eye on the rest of the company

USA (*turning round in horror*) The durned fools! They've gotten themselves all mixed up.

USSR They've disobeyed orders!

UK Good Heavens—how can they tell friend from foe when they are one solid block?

First Cleaner They don't have to. That's just what they are. One solid block.

Second Cleaner Against one enemy. Just one.

All Who?

First Cleaner ⎱ *You.* ⎰ *Speaking*
Second Cleaner ⎰   ⎱ *together*

UK Us?

USA Ridiculous.

India Totally impossible.

Africa You sure talk powerful nonsense, man.

China Enemy? China is little fliend of all the world.

USSR How can we be enemy? We are their representatives.

First Cleaner Representatives?

Second Cleaner You don't represent anything or anyone.

USA We are the dooly elected representatives of . . .

Second Cleaner I repeat—you represent no-one. For centuries people like us have stood between you and your enemies and have died while you lived on.

First Cleaner For centuries you and your kind have sat on your behinds, negotiating treaties you've no intention of keeping——

Second Cleaner —renouncing arms which you've every intention of keeping——

First Cleaner —and sending men into danger which you have no intention of sharing.

Second Cleaner We repeat, you represent no-one: and the people you do not represent have had enough. We have given you this last chance. It has ended like all the rest.

First Cleaner (*sitting in USSR's seat*) We will now have a real peace conference. Sit down, all of you.

USA Say, who's boss around here?

USSR I . . .

First Cleaner
Second Cleaner } (*firmly*) We are. { *Speaking together*

USA Like hell you are.

First Cleaner (*jabbing him with his pistol*) Sit down.

Second Cleaner (*jabbing USSR*) And you!

USSR (*with dangerous sibilance*) One thing you have forgotten. The Western world has only three minutes to live. At fourteen hundred hours Operation Mushroom Cloud goes into action.

All half-rise in agitation

First Cleaner Sit!

All sit

Second Cleaner You and your mushroom cloud. Children!

First Cleaner Bad, naughty children!

The Cleaners chuckle

USSR May I ask what is funny?

First Cleaner Your message was not the signal to push the button, but to begin dismantling push-button equipment all over the world.

Second Cleaner H.I. took over all nuclear bases five weeks ago.

Africa Who is this H.I.?

First Cleaner Humanity Incorporated.

UK Oh, God! The lunatic fringe again.

First Cleaner Not now. *You* are the lunatic fringe. We are the main body.

USA Who are you kidding? Nothing's been taken over by anyone. The personnel at all our bases is exactly the same as usual.

First Cleaner Exactly. Because all personnel are members of H.I., and Humanity Incorporated is going to make a slight change in the set-up.

USSR Ha! Revolution! I can tell you what revolution achieves you bourgeois little upstart. Nothing. A few years, and all are back at starting point. The rulers and the ruled.

China We, too, know all about revolutions. You kill us, others take place. Plenty folk available.

USA Revolutions don't change hooman nature.

Second Cleaner *Sit down and listen!* There is not going to be a revolution.

First Cleaner You're all so keen on talking that you never listen to anyone else. No wonder you are always declaring peace and going to war. We're going to stop that.

UK Oh, God! Not that Lysistrata lark again?

First Cleaner No, not the Lysistrata lark. That was hard on the women, too. We don't see why *they* should suffer. Now, shall I outline Plan A, or shall we use these—(*waving the pistol*)—and proceed directly to Plan B?

USA (*reluctantly*) I guess we'd better hear Plan A.

Second Cleaner If you don't, you'll be in no position to near Plan B.

USSR (*hastily*) Agreed to hear Plan A.

First Cleaner (*rising*) Good. Plan A entails no revolution, no change in the heads of state or members of the governments of any country, or the system of government of any country.

Africa ⎱ No change? ⎰ *Speaking*
India ⎰   ⎱ *together*

First Cleaner No change.

USA Waal, say, what are we arguing about for Gard's sake?

UK What *is* this Plan A?

First Cleaner We shall make one little adjustment to international law. It will ensure that we have only completed dedicated people to serve us.

Second Cleaner You notice we say "serve". Politicians always forget that they exist to serve their country.

India I protest. I am the most completely dedicated person I have ever met.

China I think and work only for my nation.

Africa For ourselves we care nothing. Willingly we'd lay down our lives. *Pro Patria Mori* and all that jazz.

USA That goes for all of us, I guess.

First Cleaner Splendid. Now tell us to what you dedicate yourselves in your dedicated lives.

USA (*with his hand on his heart*) My country.

UK Right or wrong.

Africa
India } That is so. Agreed, agreed. Okay, etc. { *Speaking together*
China

First Cleaner Those are just words. The words of a talking doll. You press its stomach and it says "My country right or wrong". You aren't even thinking.

Second Cleaner Think! What do you want for your countries?

UK Peace.

USSR Prosperity.

USA Waal, yes. I guess everything comes down to those two.

First Cleaner So. You are all in favour of peace?

Africa Of course.

India That is the sole and lovely purpose of our being here today.

First Cleaner And how far have you got?

USSR Negotiations have broken down—(*exploding*)—because of the treachery of America! (*He rises, pointing angrily*)

USA
UK (*rising and shouting at each other simul-*
Africa } *taneously*) Because of the treachery of { *Speaking*
China USSR/Africa/British Imperialists/India } *together*
India /China, etc.

Second Cleaner (*banging on the table with his pistol*) Quiet!

First Cleaner So you have failed.

All (*as before*) Because of the treachery of USA, etc., etc.

First Cleaner (*shouting above the din*) Never mind whose fault it is. You've failed.

They all look at one another, shrug, and slowly subside

USA Let us say negotiations have broken down.

UK The door is still o . . .

First Cleaner Face it! You've failed!

They look sheepishly at one another

And you were on the point of declaring war when we came in.

USSR (*truculently*) I had already declared it.

First Cleaner And you all insist on doing so?

China It is inevitable.

Africa We have all had acts of aggression committed against us.

First Cleaner Very well. That is all right. Now we will tell you of the slight alteration we are making to international law. It is on the matter of the declaration of war. (*To the Second Cleaner*) You've got that paper?

Second Cleaner Yes. (*He unrolls a paper*)

First Cleaner Read it. I will keep them covered.

Second Cleaner Humanity Incorporated decrees that in the event of war becoming inevitable, there shall be no bloodshed on either side until war has been officially declared.

USA What's so noo about that? It's always done.

First Cleaner Always?

USA Always.

First Cleaner Did you ever declare war on Vietnam?

USA (*wriggling*) Oh, waal—the sitooation in Vietnam is different.

First Cleaner Situations are always different. Henceforward, however, they will all be treated in the same way. (*To the Second Cleaner*) Continue.

Second Cleaner The formal declaration of war shall in future take a certain form.

First Cleaner Now listen. This is the crucial point.

Second Cleaner It shall be by the public execution of all members of governments concerned.

All (*rising in consternation*) Wha-a-at?

Second Cleaner The declaration of war shall be by the public execution of all members of the governments concerned. Not until executions have been carried out shall hostilities commence.

USA Execute *us*?

India Exterminate the government?

Africa I regard that as an undemocratic suggestion.

UK This is treason.

First Cleaner It's common sense. If you can't give orders to kill without first dying yourselves, you may be less quick off the mark with your push-buttons and telegrams.

Second Cleaner You might even begin to believe in the peace you talk so much about.

First Cleaner (*rising*) Very well. Now we know where we are. We need not interrupt you further. You were about to declare war when we came in. (*Putting away the pistol*) Go ahead. Declare it.

There is a pause of consternation

Why do you hesitate? No-one is going to stop you.

USA Say, hold it a minute. This needs thinking out.

Second Cleaner No. It's quite straightforward. Your executions are all arranged. They'll be carried out on the balcony immediately your decision to declare war is announced.

First Cleaner There will be no disgrace. Humanity Incorporated, assembled in the square, will know that you did your best, but failed.

Second Cleaner You'll have state funerals. No expense spared.

First Cleaner And of course your return fares will be refunded.

There is silence. The delegates look at one another nervously. Finally USA picks up his cable. He and USSR move back to their original places. The two Cleaners stand near the window

USA I've a kinda feeling that there's somethin' funny about this cable. It don't feel right to me. I guess it's a fake.

USSR Did I not say it was, brother? Mine too is a fake. (*He laughs and claps USA on the back*) I destroy it—so. (*He tears up the cable and throws the pieces in the air*)

USA Agreed, brother. (*He tears up his own cable*)

UK (*to Africa*) What about it?

Africa An exceedingly put-up job, in my opinion.
India A jolly unpleasant attempt to disrupt the harmony of this gathering.

They all tear up their cables and toss them in the air as they speak. USA rises emotionally to address them

USA Friends, you will forgive me if I am overcome by the sense of history we are creating. Along the walls of the corridors of time, our ancestors look down and bless us. "Courage," they say, "you have achieved what man has hoped for, but never attained."
All (*murmuring*) Hear, hear.
USSR (*rising*) Forgive me too if my emotion chokes me. For the first time in history, men have put aside envy, hatred, and all uncharitableness.
UK Never before have so few brought peace to so many. In the words of our immortal bard:
"In peace, there's nothing so becomes a man
  As modest stillness and humility.
  But when the blast of war blows in our ears . . ."
USA (*irritably*) For Chrissake, man. There's not gonna *be* any goddam blast!
UK Oh, er, I beg your pardon. I got carried away. (*He sits*)
USSR (*rising*) In Russia we have a saying, "When the samovar boils over it is time to put out the fire." This we have done. We nearly boiled over, isn't it so, but now the fire is quenched, suspicion and fear are at an end.
India We trust one another tremendously and like nobody's business, dear old boy.
China I tlust you and you tlust me. Thought number sixty-three.
Africa I would like to sing a song consisting entirely of those beautiful words.
All Later, brother, later.
USSR Gentlemen, are we ready, after this meeting so full of mutual love, trust and sincerity, to sign this treaty renouncing all wars and weapons?
All We are ready.

As the delegates sign, the two Cleaners open the window at the back and throw up their arms as if to signal the crowd outside.

*Immediately a great wave of cheering is heard, mingled with strains
of Beethoven's "Ode to Joy"*

*Before the delegates have finished signing, both doors burst
open to admit the reporters and cameramen. They gather round
the table shouting all together*

Commentators
Reporters } (*waving a microphone*) Would you care, sir, to say a few words to the world, etc. { *Speaking together*

Photographer One minute, please. A picture. And another. (*His
camera flashes*)

Second Photographer Of the actual signing. Pens in hand, please.
Thank you. And another. (*His camera flashes*)

*The delegates are photographed amid the hubbub, arms round
shoulders, or warmly shaking hands, with the same terrifying smiles
with which they started. On the noise and confusion—*

the CURTAIN *falls*

FURNITURE AND PROPERTY LIST

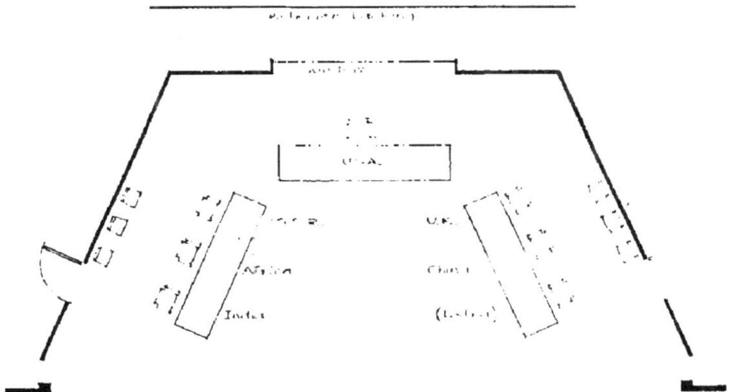

On stage: 3 long tables
1 ornate chair
6 small chairs plus others as required
Above window: cut-out of dove of peace
Around outside of window: national flags

Off stage: 7 ash-trays (**Cleaners**)
7 name-plates in trays (**Cleaners**)
Cameras and flash-bulbs (**Photographers**)
Telegrams (**Official**)
2 pistols (**Cleaners**)
Rolled document (**Second Cleaner**)

Persónal: **China:** Mao booklet
UK: notes
All Delegates: pens, folders, documents
USSR: radio pen

LIGHTING PLOT

Property fittings required: nil
A conference room

To open: General effect of daylight
No cues

EFFECTS PLOT

Cue 1   As CURTAIN rises   (Page 1)
Sprightly music

Cue 2   As **Cleaners** finish placing name-plates   (Page 1)
Cheering outside. Music changes to:
    1. African style
    2. Indian style
    3. "Star Spangled Banner"
    4. Eastern style
    5. "God Save the Queen"
    6. The "Internationale"

Cue 3   As doors are shut   (Page 3)
Cheering and music dies away

Cue 4   **Cleaners** throw up their arms   (Page 20)
Cheering and music of Beethoven's "Ode to Joy"

MADE AND PRINTED IN GREAT BRITAIN BY
LATIMER TREND & COMPANY LTD PLYMOUTH

MADE IN ENGLAND

9 780573 122750